FIRST STEAMBOAT DOWN THE MISSISSIPPI

By George S. Fichter
Illustrated by Joe Boddy

Pelican Publishing Company

GRETNA 1989

Library of Congress Cataloging-in-Publication Data

Fichter, George S.
First steamboat down the Mississippi / by George S. Fichter ;
illustrated by Joe Boddy.
     p.   cm.
Summary: A fictional account of the eventful 1811 voyage
down the Ohio and Mississippi Rivers on the steamboat "New
Orleans," told through the eyes of a fourteen-year-old deckhand.
ISBN 0-88289-715-2
[1. New Orleans (Steamboat)—Fiction. 2. Mississippi
River—Fiction.] I. Boddy, Joe, ill. II. Title.
PZ7.F44435Fi 1989
[Fic]—dc19   88-30308
                                                          CIP
                                                           AC

Manufactured in the United States of America
Published by Pelican Publishing Company, Inc.
1101 Monroe Street, Gretna, Louisiana 70053

CONTENTS

For Julia

FIRST STEAMBOAT DOWN THE MISSISSIPPI

INTRODUCTION

THE STRANGE YEAR OF 1811

Many people believed the Great Comet was responsible for the unusual happenings of 1811. First
sighted in France, the giant comet left a fiery trail
around the world.

The only records of what the comet looked like
were made on artists' canvases. Their brushes show
it as a brilliant ball of fire trailing two bright tails
that, astronomers now calculate, were longer than
the distance from the earth to the sun. The comet
itself is estimated to have been more than fifteen
million miles wide.

Wineries in Portugal that year turned out the best
wine in their history. Called Comet Wine, it sold for
a much higher price than wines they made earlier or
for years to come. But elsewhere in the world, people
believed the fiery object in the sky brought little
good. Its persistence was eerie. Sometimes the

streaking comet could be seen all night long—and for week after week.

The year 1811 ended in the United States with the most powerful earthquake ever known on the North American continent. Like the Great Comet, which superstitious people considered to be the cause of all such catastrophes, the earthquake seemed to have no ending. Tremors continued, in fact, until the spring of the following year. Day after day the earth trembled. Great chasms opened in the earth's surface. Whole forests were swallowed, and lakes were created where once there were hills.

Tim Collins, the boy in the story on the following pages, lived in this year filled with disasters, triumphs, and adventures. Tim is fictional, but the rest of the story is based on fact. The *New Orleans* was indeed the first steamboat to travel the Mississippi. And what a year to have made that first trip!

CHAPTER ONE

IT BEGAN IN PITTSBURGH

Tim Collins lay stretched on his stomach in a grassy pocket between two giant rocks on top of Boyd's Hill. From here, high on the bluff, he could see all of Pittsburgh sprawled along the east bank of the Monongahela River where it joined the Allegheny. But Tim was most interested in what was happening directly below him.

Where a creek had flooded the low land behind an iron foundry, men were wading through the shallow, roiled waters busily snaking out fresh-cut lumber and carrying it back to higher ground. There they stacked it near the ribwork of a mighty boat. Judging from its skeleton, Tim guessed the boat would measure more than a hundred feet long from prow to stern. Tim had never seen a boat that big. He needed work, and maybe this was where he could get it.

Tim pushed up with his arms and sprang to his

feet. Almost fifteen, he was lithe as a cat, his muscles wiry from work. He began half-running and half-sliding down the slope toward the shipyard. How strange, he thought to himself, that he now expected something good to happen due to a flood, for it was the swollen, rampaging waters of the Allegheny that had dealt him trouble earlier this year.

All of 1811 had so far been unusual—and for Tim, tragic. The year had begun with a fiery comet that rode across the dark winter sky. Tim's father and mother had talked about what the appearance of the ghostlike comet meant. Many people believed it was a signal that the world would soon come to an end. Tim's mother searched the Bible for an explanation of the eerie ball of fire.

Soon after the comet came, the winter turned unusually warm. Rains melted the heavy snows that blanketed the land. Little streams became rushing torrents that fed the big rivers, and the big rivers rose higher and higher until they spilled over their banks and swept through the low country.

Tim's father had built their cabin on a rise of ground near the Allegheny River. He had cleared the rich bottomland all around it to plant corn, pumpkins, and other food crops. As the river rose, the little hill on which the cabin sat became an island. Tim and his father drove stakes into the ground back from the water's edge and watched hour by hour as the river continued to rise steadily. Finally it reached the stakes.

Staying in the cabin was no longer safe. Using the cabin door, they made a raft on which to float themselves and a few belongings to higher ground. In the hills high above the river, they found a cave where they decided to stay until the river settled back into its banks. Then they could go back to their cabin.

But the big cave was cold and damp. They were not able to warm it with fires, and the weather outside grew worse rather than better. The rain turned first into wet snow, then sleet, and finally back to rain again. A dense fog filled the valley between the hills and came into the cave as a wet, dripping cloud. Accompanying the bad weather was a flu epidemic that swept through the country, and Tim's father and mother became ill. The same illness kept their few and distant neighbors from coming to help—or even to see how they had fared the flood.

One night Tim's father died. Tim made a coffin for him from the remains of the raft and then buried him in a quiet meadow below the cave. For two weeks longer Tim cared for his mother as well as he could, but each day she grew worse. She made Tim promise that if she died he would not stay in the cold mountain country. She begged him to go to Natchez far down the Mississippi where he could live with her sister. And there it would be warm.

Until her voice became too weak, she read aloud from the Bible every day. During her last days, Tim did the reading. When she died, he put her to rest by his father, and he marked their graves with crosses made of limbs from which he peeled the bark.

Tim then set out across the hills toward Pittsburgh, a two-day journey from the cave. To get to Natchez, the easiest way was by river, first through the wilderness of the Ohio River country and then south on the Mississippi. Tim planned to find work in Pittsburgh to get enough money for the supplies he would need, and it was obvious that the men below Boyd's Hill needed help.

From the bottom of the hill, Tim hurried across the soggy bottomland to where the men were still in the water fishing out the floating lumber. Over his shoulder, Tim carried a blanket roll tied with a rope. Inside were the few belongings he brought from the cave. Tim walked directly to the burly man who was bossing the work crew.

"Need a worker, mister?" he asked.

"A man we could use," the big fellow barked gruffly. "A boy, no."

Tim cringed. Being a boy was something he could not help, but he knew he could do a man's work. "I'll give you a day's work," he snapped back boldly, brushing the shock of curly brown hair off his forehead. "When I'm done, you pay me only if you agree that I've done as much as a man."

Tim had proposed a deal the man could not turn down. He nodded an agreement and motioned Tim to join the workers.

Tim tucked his blanket roll into the crotch of a tree to keep it off the wet ground and then plunged into the muddy water up to his knees to help drag out the lumber. Most of it was fresh-cut white pine. The other workers told him it would be used for decking on the big boat. And what he learned about the boat itself was the biggest surprise of all. It was a steamboat!

They told him the boat was being built for a man named Nicholas Roosevelt and that he planned to steam down the Ohio to the Mississippi and then continue southward to Natchez. There he would put the steamboat to work carrying cargo and passengers between Natchez and New Orleans. To be named the *New Orleans*, she would become the first steamboat to travel the waters of the West.

Steamboats were already being used on a few rivers and lakes in the East, but they were still new everywhere. Few people thought the idea of a steamboat on the Mississippi was practical. They did not believe that a steam-powered boat could possibly be powerful enough to move against the big river's strong, steady downstream current when she traveled from New Orleans up to Natchez.

But Mr. Roosevelt was convinced the steamboat could master the mighty river. First he built a flatboat and made a six-month journey covering the course his *New Orleans* would travel in getting from Pittsburgh to Natchez. He measured the speed of the river, charted the rapids and places where whirling currents might be hazardous, and calculated the best time of the year for getting the steamboat around the dangerous Falls of the Ohio just below Louisville. Wherever he could, he collected coal and wood and piled them along the shore so they could be taken aboard as the *New Orleans* steamed downstream.

After his exploration, Mr. Roosevelt went to New York to report his findings to Robert Fulton and Robert Livingston, the two men in the United States who knew most about steamboats and who had a keen interest in seeing them come into use on the rivers of the West. These two men already owned and operated steamboats on lakes and rivers in the East. They liked Mr. Roosevelt's enthusiasm and thoroughness, and they agreed to give him the money he needed to build the boat. He asked for $40,000, and now the boat was taking shape.

Tim wished Mr. Roosevelt were there now. He wanted to meet this man who was so determined to pioneer a whole new way of life for the West. But Mr. Roosevelt had gone to New York to buy machinery and to hire special mechanics for making the boat steam-powered. No one in Pittsburgh knew enough about how a Fulton steamboat operated to be able to help him.

At the end of that first day, the boss of the work crew agreed that Tim had won his point. He had worked so willingly and so hard that he could have a job helping to finish the boat. But Tim had already begun to think about what might happen when the boat was ready for its trip. He had decided he would like to become a member of the crew. This would get him to Natchez much faster than he had expected. He would be going with pay and—most exciting—on the very first steamboat to the West.

By the time Mr. Roosevelt got back from New York, the shipyard was dry again, and the *New Orleans* was almost ready for her engine. Every day the sawing and hammering had started at dawn and continued until dark. Tim first cut decking boards. Then he helped frame the big cabin with its pilot-house on top. This was located near the stern of the boat. The big cabin was divided into three parts. The forward half was for the crew. In the middle was the galley, where meals would be cooked—and also eaten when the weather was bad. Toward the stern was one large room and another only about half as large. The large room was for Mr. Roosevelt and his wife, Lydia. Much to Tim's surprise, she planned to make the journey with them. The smaller room was for Mrs. Roosevelt's maid—Mrs. Roosevelt would be having a baby sometime before they reached Natchez and would need another woman aboard to take care of her and the new child.

Tim was even more astonished when he saw the Roosevelts. They were much younger than he had expected. Mrs. Roosevelt was indeed a lady. On her first visit to the *New Orleans*, she came dressed in her finery. And Mr. Roosevelt was a richly dressed and handsome man, obviously accustomed to the best in style.

But Tim's awe turned to respect when he watched the Roosevelts check the *New Orleans*. Because of their elegance, every move they made commanded attention, yet they were genuine and kindly, speaking with familiarity to all of the workers. Mr. Roosevelt called most of them by name, and his voice was firm and authoritative. He knew exactly what he wanted and also how to get the workers to produce it.

When their tour brought them to where Tim was working, Mr. Roosevelt quickly recognized him as a new worker. "When did you hire this young chap?" Mr. Roosevelt asked the boss.

The shipbuilder told Mr. Roosevelt how Tim had offered his services free if he did not work as well as any man, and he added that every day Tim had proved his worth. Tim smiled in appreciation. Now was his chance, he believed, and so he came out with his request almost before he had time to think exactly how to put it in words.

"Sir," he addressed Mr. Roosevelt, "I am on my way to Natchez. I would be pleased to sign on the *New Orleans* as a member of the crew."

"Do you know riverboating?" Mr. Roosevelt asked.

"No," Tim answered honestly, "but I am a hard worker and am quick to learn. Besides, it would be a pity for you to have to get somebody else when I am going that way anyhow."

Mr. Roosevelt laughed at Tim's directness. He stroked his chin thoughtfully for a moment and then said, "Boy, you've got your way to Natchez on the *New Orleans.* You will have plenty to eat, a place to sleep, and a stake of money when we get there." He reached out and shook Tim's hand to confirm the deal.

"Thank you, sir," Tim managed to say. It had happened so fast he could hardly believe it was true.

"Go to Bull's Inn this evening and tell Jack Fitch that I said you are a member of his crew. He is the captain of the *New Orleans,* and you will be directly responsible to him," Mr. Roosevelt said. He and Mrs. Roosevelt then moved on. She wanted to inspect the cabin that she and her husband would occupy during the trip.

"Back at it, boy," Tim heard the boss man commanding him. Tim suddenly realized that he had been standing motionless for several minutes while thoughts of the strange happenings in his life spun through his mind. Quickly he grabbed a hammer and began to fit plank to plank on the deck. He knew now he would be walking on this deck all the way to Natchez.

That evening Tim scrubbed up in the creek behind the shipyard. With the big comb that had belonged to his mother, he straightened the tangles from his wet hair. Then he headed for Bull's Inn to meet Captain Fitch.

As he approached the inn, which stood at a crossroads on the edge of Pittsburgh, Tim could hear the loud voices and laughter inside. He pushed the door open cautiously. The room was dark and smoky. Tim stood quietly for a few minutes to give his eyes time to adjust to the darkness.

Bull's Inn was the gathering place for rivermen in Pittsburgh. They were a rough and rowdy group. One of them spied Tim in the doorway.

"Lookit the young-un!" he roared. "We throw that size back into the river."

Others joined him in guffawing.

Now Tim could see them clearly. Some were traders and trappers who had come to Bull's Inn to get riverboatmen to take them to the West. The riverboatmen were a breed of their own. They were the lords of the river, and here at Bull's Inn they did their bragging—and some of their fighting.

"What's for you, boy?" the innkeeper bellowed.

"Jack Fitch, sir. I'm looking for Captain Fitch."

Again the men laughed. "*Captain* Fitch," they parroted. Tim heard them making snide remarks about Jack Fitch's fancy title now that he was becoming a steamboater.

"I'm Jack Fitch," a tall, smiling, muscular young

man said as he stepped forward. "What kin I do for you?"

Tim heard the twang that marked Jack Fitch as a Kentuckian, and he was relieved that he seemed to be so friendly. "Mr. Roosevelt sent me, sir," Tim said. "He told me to tell you that I am a member of your crew."

At this the men in Bull's Inn let loose uncontrolled laughter.

"That man Roosevelt sure is a dandy," one said. "First he gets this crazy notion about running a steamboat on the big river, and now he sends you a boy for your crew. Hey, Fitch, you sure enough better take you plenty of poles to shove your way along. You're gonna need 'em. And that boy ain't likely to be much help when it comes to real riverboatin'."

"Hold your tongue about Mr. Roosevelt," Jack Fitch said sharply. And to give meaning to his words the only way riverboatmen could understand, he hoisted the man off the bench where he was sitting and flat-handed him, sending him sprawling into a corner of the room. Then he stood in crouched readiness to carry on the fight if needed.

Jack Fitch stood six feet four inches tall in his moccasins. He was as broad across his shoulders as the beam of a canoe and as thin-waisted as the prow. Bull's Inn became suddenly quiet; nobody moved. The man on the floor muttered a bit, but he stayed where he was, wisely figuring that a second trip would be less comfortable than the first.

Jack Fitch relaxed his taut muscles and turned back to Tim. "Come outside, boy. We'd best talk a bit."

Tim liked Jack Fitch. He was obviously a man of loyalty and principles, and he had the muscles to defend what he believed was right. He asked Tim how he had gotten to know Mr. Roosevelt and why he had been selected as a crew member. Picking crew members, he explained, was really his job. But when Tim told him how it happened, he was completely satisfied. It was clear that he shared Tim's confidence in Mr. Roosevelt.

"Boy," Captain Fitch said, putting his hand on Tim's shoulder, "by the time we get to Natchez, you'll be one of the best riverboatmen in the West— and with steamboatin' under your belt, too. You are a lucky lad. Maybe you'll bring us luck, too. Could be we'll need it. And boy, you don't have to be so formal and call me Captain Fitch—Captain Jack will do fine," he added with a grin.

Tim walked back to the shipyard. He had been sleeping in a shed at the back of the iron foundry, but tonight he boarded the *New Orleans* and bedded down in the cabin that would be his home all the way to Natchez.

CHAPTER TWO

A SURPRISE VISITOR

"Wake up, boy!"

Jack Fitch prodded Tim with his boot. At the first touch Tim sprang to his feet in the early morning's dimness.

"Something wrong?" he mumbled, thinking first that he should have asked before taking it upon himself to sleep aboard the *New Orleans*.

"Nothing you can't manage when you get yourself awake," Captain Jack responded. "We just got to get things cleaned up and in order early today. Mr. Latrobe's in town and will be payin' us a visit."

"Who?" Tim was wide awake now, but the name Latrobe meant nothing to him.

"Latrobe. Latrobe," Jack Fitch repeated. "Lydia's father."

"He lives around here?"

"No, boy. Came in last night from Washington. You mean you've never heard of Ben Latrobe?

Where've you been? Lydia Roosevelt's father—that's Ben Latrobe—is one of the most important men in the country. He's a real somebody."

"In what way?" Tim asked.

"Well, he's what they call an architect. Decides how a building's supposed to look, draws up the plans, and then makes sure it's done that way. He's the man that built the big Bank of Pennsylvania in Philadelphia. Never seen it myself, but I hear tell it's the most beautiful building in the country. Did a lot of other buildings in Philadelphia, too, including some churches.

"He's also an engineer. He did the Philadelphia Waterworks. It uses steam engines to pump the water. That's how he got to know Mr. Roosevelt, who was building steam engines over in New Jersey at the time. And that's when Mr. Roosevelt met Lydia. She was mighty young when he first saw her. He watched her grow up into the fine lady she is now.

"Like her father, Lydia was born in England. Her mother died when Lydia was only a couple of years old, and Mr. Latrobe left her in England with an aunt until he got settled here in the United States and was married again. Then he sent for her and her brother."

"Does Mr. Latrobe still do buildings?" Tim asked.

"Sure does. Right now, in fact, he's still at work on buildings in Washington. He went there when President Jefferson asked him to design the Capitol, then he stayed on to do other government buildings. They tell me he did some additions to the President's House, too.

"He's interested in more than buildings, though.

Does paintings, too, and steam engines really fasci-
nate him, Mr. Roosevelt says. He has done some
work with Robert Fulton, just like Mr. Roosevelt.
He's stopping here to have a look at the *New Orleans*
before we get the steam engine aboard. Then he'll be
taking a trip to New Orleans where he has been
asked to build a steam-operated waterworks like the
one he did in Philadelphia. 'Course this is a chance
for him to see Lydia, too, before she starts her trip
and before she gives birth to his second grandchild."

"Second grandchild?" Tim echoed. He was surprised to find out the Roosevelts had another child.

"Sure," Jack Fitch continued. "Their first is a
little girl just a mite over a year old now. Her name
is Rosetta Mark. Lydia left her in Philadelphia with
a close friend—the one she was named after."

It was light enough now for Tim to set about getting the *New Orleans* in shape for their visitor. Captain Jack said he would keep the crew and workers
at Bull's Inn until Mr. Latrobe left.

While he worked, Tim went over in his mind what
Jack Fitch had told him about Lydia Roosevelt. Now
he understood why she seemed to be someone very
special, for indeed she was. She was much more than
just young, beautiful, and outgoing. She had un-
common courage and determination that set her on
a course others would have been fearful to follow.
Her bravery and pioneering spirit were inborn, and
her desire to give birth to a baby on the first trip ever
made by steamboat down the Ohio and Mississippi
rivers seemed ordained.

Long before the sun was high in the heavens, Tim
had the *New Orleans* as cleaned up as if she were

going to be sold. He had begun putting things in order in the storage shed they had built on the shore when he noticed Tiger, Mrs. Roosevelt's big Newfoundland dog. Tiger, who would be taking the trip with them, had apparently been wandering in the brush nearby and gotten into a patch of burs. They were thick in his coat and even on the pads of his paws. He was trying to pull them out with his teeth, but they kept digging into his muzzle and gums, making matters worse. He whimpered in pain.

Tim knelt beside the big dog and began pulling out burs. Here and there he had to cut whole patches from Tiger's coat because the burs were too entangled in the fur to get them out one by one. Tiger seemed to understand that Tim was giving him the help he needed. He wagged his tail as he watched, and he did not object when Tim turned him over or stretched out a leg to get at a batch of burs. Tim talked to the big dog all the while. Neither he nor Tiger noticed Lydia Roosevelt coming up behind them.

Lydia like the way Tim had taken to Tiger. The two got along as though Tiger really belonged to Tim, yet whenever she appeared, Tim always told Tiger to go to her. He was not at all possessive.

"How kind of you," Lydia said appreciatively.

"Thank you," Tim replied in his usual respectful tone. From the first time he saw her, Tim had felt a closeness to Lydia. Now that he knew more about her, his respect was even greater.

Lydia had taken a special liking to Tim, too. From her husband she had learned why he was working on the *New Orleans.* She knew about the loss of his parents during the flu epidemic the previous winter. Because she had lost her mother, she felt she understood his feelings better than most people. She admired Tim's determination to carry out his mother's wish that he find his aunt in Natchez, and she told her husband they should do all they could to be of help.

"Mr. Roosevelt and I sincerely hope you do locate your aunt in Natchez," she said, "but in case she has moved on, please consider us your family until you get settled."

Tim smiled. "Nothing could please me more," he said honestly. "I will not abuse the offer, but I will never forget it."

"You may decide to come back to Pennsylvania," Lydia went on. "My father will be coming to New Orleans more than once on business. You could travel back with him. He will probably go by ship from New Orleans through the Gulf of Mexico and then up the Atlantic coast."

All Tim could muster was another smile and a shake of his head. He did not plan to be traveling with Mr. Latrobe, of course. He was confident he would find his aunt in Natchez and would be living with her. But it meant a great deal to know that Mr. Roosevelt thought so highly of him.

At that point there came a shout from the path leading to the *New Orleans*. It was Mr. Roosevelt.

"Lydia! Lydia!" he called. "We have company."

With Mr. Roosevelt was a tall, distinguished, dark-haired man. Tim could see in him a likeness to Lydia, who began moving quickly toward the men. Tim went into the storage shed to straighten it up and busy himself, keeping politely out of the way.

He could hear the three of them as they walked along the deck. Mr. Roosevelt was explaining every detail about the construction of the *New Orleans*, and he was getting a lot of questions from Mr. Latrobe.

"She's ready now for the engine," Tim heard Mr. Roosevelt say. "We'll have that installed soon, and we expect to be on our way before winter sets in."

They moved on to inspect the cabin the Roosevelts would occupy during the trip. Meanwhile Jack Fitch had gone aboard the boat, too, and Tim heard Mr. Latrobe asking him questions about the river. Obviously he wanted to see how well Jack Fitch knew the waters they would be traveling. His interest in the *New Orleans* was more than casual. He said he was considering investing in Fulton's projects in New York, and there was a chance he might get involved, too, with Mr. Roosevelt in his Mississippi venture.

Tim was so busy that he did not hear them leave the *New Orleans.* He was surprised when suddenly they were there in the shed with him.

"I want you to meet the youngest member of our crew," Mr. Roosevelt said with a smile. And then he turned to Tim. "This is Mr. Benjamin Latrobe, my wife's father."

"I have heard much about you, sir," Tim said. "I am honored to meet you."

"But I have probably heard much more about you," Ben Latrobe replied. "They tell me you are hard working, kind, intelligent, and determined. I can't imagine anyone having more admirable qualities."

Tim was pleased but embarrassed. He shifted from one foot to the other, not really knowing how to respond to such compliments. Ben Latrobe recognized that he had overwhelmed the boy.

"Lydia tells me you are on the way to Natchez," he went on. "She also told me that if your mission there does not work out as you hope then you might want to come back to Pennsylvania. I'd appreciate being able to travel with you—if you can wait until I get there and finish a bit of business."

Tim grinned. What an unusual way to invite him to be his companion. "I'll wait for you," he said. "At this point, though, I really think I will be staying with my aunt in Natchez."

He shook hands with Mr. Latrobe and wished him a good trip. The Roosevelts and Mr. Latrobe then walked away, heading back to the inn where they were staying. As they left, Lydia glanced over her shoulder and gave Tim a parting smile.

Tim had just passed another test.

CHAPTER THREE

THEY'RE OFF

The *New Orleans* now looked like a boat, but she was not ready for launching. Still to be installed was the machinery—a big boiler that would furnish the steam to drive the engine and wheels. When this was done, the *New Orleans* would look like no other boat ever seen in Pittsburgh.

Crowds gathered at the shipyard every day to watch the work progress, and now Tim saw Mr. Roosevelt's skill in action. He had worked with Robert Fulton in building his steamboats that were now competing successfully against sailing schooners on trips up the Hudson River to Albany. So Mr. Roosevelt knew the workings of steamboats as well as the man he had brought from New York to help him.

The *New Orleans* was a new design made by Mr. Fulton. Its big boiler, located midships, would generate the steam to push a thirty-four-inch piston

for turning two large paddlewheels, one on each side of the boat. From the firebox, a stack rose fifteen feet above the deck. The wheel in the pilothouse of the *New Orleans* was located just over the stern and connected directly to the rudder for turning the boat. At night or in bad weather, signals would be called from the prow by a crewman or pilot so that the helmsman could steer the boat properly.

Tim helped get all of the machinery aboard and watched while Mr. Roosevelt and the New York engineer put the pieces in place. All during these days Mr. Roosevelt worked from dawn until dark. He did not wear his fancy clothes, but even so, he stood out as different from the others. He could not hide those qualities that set him apart from the crew.

Everyone who came to the shipyard to watch had words of wisdom to pass along. Most of them were discouraging. Almost no one believed that a steamboat would be able to push against the strong current of the Mississippi on runs from New Orleans to Natchez. Neither did they think the *New Orleans* would ever have a chance to try, for they did not believe the steamboat would get past the Falls of the Ohio. Some predicted that the boiler would explode even before the steamboat got to Cincinnati. Others advised people to stand clear when the boiler was fired up right there in Pittsburgh.

Nearly every day, as the time drew nearer for the *New Orleans* to depart, somebody came to talk to Mr. Roosevelt about his wife. No matter what, most of them declared, the West was no place for a woman of such refinement. The hazards of a trip such as the

New Orleans was about to take were simply too great for a woman, and it was absolutely unthinkable to allow her to go on the trip when she was expecting a child. They begged him to leave Mrs. Roosevelt in Pittsburgh on this first trip. He could return for her and for his child if the trip was successful.

It was Mrs. Roosevelt who insisted on going, however. She said she would not even consider letting the *New Orleans* leave Pittsburgh without her. And if Mr. Roosevelt ever questioned her taking the trip, he did not show it. His wife's absolute confidence in his ability was all he needed to drive him onward to success.

Meanwhile Captain Jack had set about hiring his crew. He needed five more to add to Tim, and the five he selected were all burly rivermen. The New York engineer signed on to run the steam engine. A cook was hired, and they agreed to pick up pilots as needed along the way. These would be men who knew particular stretches of the river especially well.

Tiger, Mrs. Roosevelt's dog, was to take the trip, too. He was a gentle, sad-eyed giant, but because of his keen eyes and ears, he would be depended on to alert them to dangers on the journey. Tim and the big dog had become fast friends, so Tim was happy they would be making the voyage together.

About the middle of September, Mr. Roosevelt announced that it was time to give the *New Orleans* her first trial. The creek was as high as it would be for a long while, and they might have no opportunity later to get the big boat afloat. The *New Orleans* was sitting on long rollers at the creek's wide mouth, and sliding her down the bank into the water was no problem. She splashed into the water, wobbled a bit despite her twenty-foot beam, then righted herself and floated steadily.

Tim and the crew helped get the paddlewheels in position so that Mr. Roosevelt and the engineer could connect them to the engine's driving arm. Mr. Roosevelt then promised that the very next day, bright and early, they would fire the boiler to test the engine. If all went well, they would put the *New Orleans* through her first paces.

That night Tim could hardly sleep. Mostly it was because he was excited, but there was another reason, too. Tim had been sleeping aboard the *New Orleans*, a night watchman's duty that he had taken upon himself, but tonight the boat was on the water. All night long the *New Orleans* rocked gently, and Tim listened to the sound of the current slapping against her sides. This is what it will be like every night on the journey to Natchez, he told himself. But no, the engine noise would be too loud. Or would they travel at night? Maybe the engine would be shut down. All of a sudden Tim was asking himself many questions about the trip. He wondered what it would be like when the big piston began to turn the wheels in water—and he would soon know.

Before sunup the next morning, Mr. Roosevelt and the engineer were aboard the *New Orleans* and had a fire going under the boiler to build a head of steam. Thick black coal smoke curled out of the stack and drifted down the valley. It caught the eyes of passers-by, who stopped to learn what was happening. Before the morning was well started, a crowd had gathered along the creek. Those still believing that an explosion was likely stayed what they hoped was a safe distance back from the boat. Tim worked closely with Mr. Roosevelt and the engineer, feeding the fire when necessary and making last minute checks on the machinery.

Finally Mr. Roosevelt turned a valve at the side of the boiler, and a cloud of steam rushed out with a loud hissing noise. The crowd gasped. They thought for certain the boiler was blowing up. Mr. Roosevelt chuckled.

"She's ready now," he announced. "Let's give her the test."

Captain Jack and his crew untied the lines that held the *New Orleans* to the shore and pushed her out into the wide, deep water. This was a magic moment, and no one talked. Everyone turned his eyes toward the engineer who would pull the lever allowing the great piston to push the paddlewheels. Meanwhile, with their poles, the crew had gotten the *New Orleans* out into the middle of the river, and she was drifting slowly downstream with the current. But she was turned so that she was drifting stern first.

"Let the wheels roll!" Captain Jack shouted.

Mr. Roosevelt nodded his assent.

The engineer grabbed the long lever and pulled it down. First came a sharp grinding noise and then a screeching as parts that had never moved before began to turn. Then the big wheels themselves began to roll through the water.

A great cheer came from the crowd on shore as the

New Orleans stopped her downstream drift and then, almost seeming to strain, began to move upstream against the current. As the boat moved back past the people on shore, Mr. Roosevelt and his crew waved. They churned on upstream to the first bend, then turned her around and came back. With the current helping to push them, they seemed to fly past the people on shore.

Mr. Roosevelt had Captain Jack turn the *New Orleans* around and go upstream once more. Now the screaming parts in the engine had quieted down. Rough edges had been worn away, and grease had worked its way between parts that rubbed. The only noise now was the rhythmic pounding thrust of the piston and the sound of the water being carried upward by the wheels. It reminded Tim of the wheel at the gristmill where he used to go with his father to have their corn ground into meal. The only difference was that the *New Orleans* had two and larger wheels.

Word had spread through Pittsburgh that the steamboat was being tested, and three times as many people now stood on the shore watching the *New Orleans* being put through her paces.

"She's running with full power," the engineer shouted to Mr. Roosevelt.

And indeed she was. It was spectacular.

Captain Jack told Tim he'd wager they were going upstream at eight miles an hour or even faster. "Sure beats polin'," he said with a satisfied smile. He stood, arms folded, watching the *New Orleans* plow past flatboats that were struggling laboriously against the current.

The *New Orleans* had proved herself. Now it was time to make final preparations for the big trip down the river. All of Pittsburgh now buzzed about the steamboat. People came from miles around to see the unusual boat before she left the area. Still the skeptics pointed out that the most critical test had not been passed. The Monongahela River was far from being as strong as the Mississippi. They still doubted that the *New Orleans* would be a match for the big river's might.

Mr. Roosevelt did not waste time arguing. If pressed for comment, he suggested that anyone who doubted what the *New Orleans* could do should hurry on down to Natchez. They might get there in time to buy passage for the first trip from Natchez to New Orleans and back. Mr. Roosevelt was much more concerned about getting ready for the trip than talking about it. He wanted to be certain they were well down the Mississippi River before the winter freezes came.

Every morning a fire was built under the boiler. As soon as steam hissed out of the safety valve, the *New Orleans* was pushed offshore for a quick run up and down the river. Each practice run made the crew more confident—more skilled in handling the big boat and more comfortable in knowing what she could do. At Bull's Inn, the crew now talked boastfully about how they would pass the flatboats both coming and going.

September was nearly over when Mr. Roosevelt announced one morning that the *New Orleans* would be leaving in just two days. During those last hours, he and his wife were treated to farewell get-togethers by all their friends in Pittsburgh. Many people still tried to persuade Mrs. Roosevelt to stay in the Pittsburgh area until the *New Orleans* reached Natchez safely. Again they warned her of the hardships of the river, of the pirates and outlaws who preyed on river traffic and who would be delighted to have a charming female victim, and of the still hostile Indians who lived in the wilderness of the West and who would surely attack the big boat. They concocted tales about all the dangers they had ever heard about, quite unaware that Nature had more unusual happenings in the offing for the year 1811 than they could imagine.

On the day the *New Orleans* set out for Cincinnati, it seemed that everyone in Pittsburgh lined the shore to see her off. As the big boat's wheels churned the water, Captain Jack spun the wheel to head her into the main channel. The people shouted, tossed hats into the air, and waved their arms. The women cried at the thought of beautiful Mrs. Roosevelt, about to have a baby and going bravely on the trip just to be with her husband. The men cheered. Caught up with the spirit of adventure, many of them now wished they were aboard. Older people shook their heads in disbelief at the floating, hissing furnace. What could the world be coming to with such a noisy, smoky boat more powerful than the river itself? Surely the devil had a hand in this somewhere.

Tim had been a part of the *New Orleans* now from her early days, but he could not believe himself that this was not just a dream. When all the lines were in, he watched the cluster of people on shore until they had shrunk to tiny figures. With the *New Orleans* now no more than a spot on the river, the crowd began to break up. Tim watched. Those people were no longer a part of his dream. He was riding on his dream, in fact, and it would be his home all the way to Cincinnati, then to Louisville, and finally Natchez. Again he wondered if it was as real as it seemed.

A big black horsefly landed on his leg, and a few seconds later he felt a sharp, stabbing pain as the fly stuck its stilettolike beak through his skin. He slapped the fly, and blood spurted from the wound. Tim was sure then that this was no dream.

At almost the same instant he heard Captain Jack calling to him. "Tim, take a pole position on the starboard."

And that was no dream, either. All of this, in fact, was very real.

Tim grabbed a pole from the rail and took his post on the right side of the boat just behind the prow. His job was to watch for logs or other objects and to push them away from the boat. With the help of another crewman on the left side, he was to make certain the boat followed the main channel. This was a job Tim would have daily on the trip down the river.

The *New Orleans* traveled swiftly down the Ohio and around a bend. Pittsburgh was out of sight. On each side the sharp peaks of the Allegheny foothills poked into the September sky. At the next turn, the *New Orleans* seemed to be cruising directly into the sunset.

CHAPTER FOUR

DOWN THE RIVER TO CINCINNATI

On the first night of the voyage to Cincinnati, no one aboard the *New Orleans* could sleep. Most did not even try. Everyone was wide awake, getting a fill of the magic of the steamboat.

Mr. Roosevelt did not ordinarily plan to travel at night. Just before dark they would tie up along shore, leaving time while it was light to take on fuel or to get supplies aboard if they were near a settlement. But sometimes he would make an exception.

A giant autumn moon had turned the river into a silvery ribbon that wormed between the bushy, forested hills. It was almost as bright as daylight, yet the yellowness made the night mystic and things seemed only half-real. It was a warm late September night, but driven along by both steam and river current, the *New Orleans* moved fast enough so that the air felt refreshingly cool.

"She's doing eight to maybe ten miles an hour, I

figure," Captain Jack announced to Mr. Roosevelt.

"Fine, fine," Mr. Roosevelt answered. He and the engineer checked the engine from time to time to make certain it was working properly.

"She steers beautifully," Captain Jack volunteered a bit later. He felt that the *New Orleans* was operating even better than on the test runs at Pittsburgh. This was new water running under the steamboat's keel.

Tim sat hunched close to the starboard rail near the prow. It was not his turn on duty, but like the others, he was drinking his fill of the ride. Now and then a shift in the wind would carry the column of smoke from the stack across the moon's face like a skinny black cloud. Behind him the piston churned rhythmically. On each side of the boat the big wheels rolled through the water, and streams of silvery water trailed off the paddles and into the river behind them. Great flocks of ducks and geese were sometimes startled from their rest on the river, and now and then a fish skipped across the water in front of them.

Time after time the *New Orleans* overtook flatboats drifting quietly with the current. For the sport of it, the engineer would fire up the *New Orleans* just before they got to the boat. As they went by, sparks would be flying from the billowing smokestack. Dozing riverboatmen would be jolted wide awake. They would heave on their poles and shove the rudder of their flatboat to the port or the starboard, whichever direction was surer to get them out of the way of the steamboat. The crew aboard the *New Orleans* kept quiet so they could hear what the riverboatmen said.

"What in tarnation is *that?*" was the usual. The question came in different forms and was often punctuated with cursing when the riverboatman thought he was being run down by some belching monster.

Many of the flatboats and rafts that the *New Orleans* overtook had started in Pittsburgh, and their occupants knew about this boat.

"I'll be hornbuckled. Thar's Mr. Roosevelt's boat. She's done made it."

If they knew members of the crew, they called out their names. Captain Jack seemed to know everybody on the river, for he had traveled the Ohio River by flatboat many times himself. Tim was amazed at the way Captain Jack followed the river channel when there were no markings. He knew every twist and turn the way a person learns his house so well he can walk through it in the dark without stumbling.

Tim stood by Captain Jack at the wheel for a while.

"You have to know the river four ways, Tim," Captain Jack told him. "She looks one way going downstream but the same places look entirely different when you come at them from the other direction. Then you also have to know the river both by day and by night."

Tim watched Captain Jack spin the wheel to follow a swing of the channel from the north shore toward the south.

"The river changes with the seasons, too," Captain Jack went on. "Right now the water's deep almost all the way down to Cincinnati. We'll have no trouble. When we hit a long dry spell, then we get shoals.

Never would have risked running the river at night when it was low."

Captain Jack talked on about how you could read the river. "See how deep the shadows are over toward the shore?" he asked, pointing to an inky blackness that had fallen over the river where it was now out of the direct moonlight. "You can't even see the shoreline, but that's where the deep water is. I can tell from the strength of the current."

Captain Jack steered the *New Orleans* into a darkness that to Tim had looked like the shore itself. But the wheels churned through deep water.

"Over there in the moonlight," Captain Jack went on, "the water's only a few inches deep in spots. It runs over a flatrock bed that could cut the bottom from under us. Bend down and you can see where the water bumps on a high rock now and then. You can see little white caps of foam on the surface."

Tim understood now more than ever before why Mr. Roosevelt had chosen Jack Fitch to skipper the *New Orleans* down the river. The job called for a man whose head was filled with facts about the river and how to navigate it.

"Soon we'll come to a spot where an old snag has caught a whole jam of driftwood. Some of them have got hung up quite a piece out into the river. We'll have to head back toward the north shore and edge around them."

Only a man who knew every inch of the river as Captain Jack did would have dared take the *New Orleans* downstream at such a fast pace at night.

Tim moved to the stern, where he sat watching the moon-flecked water in the wake of the boat. The shimmering silver took him away from the world in which he was living at the moment. For the first time in months, Tim's thoughts drifted back to his home and his father and mother. He remembered his father telling about how he and Tim's mother had traveled across the Atlantic in a sailing vessel. Tim's journey on the *New Orleans* was not exactly the same, of course, but now Tim was on a boat, too, traveling to a new life as they had done.

The ship that brought them across the Atlantic from England was really not much larger than the *New Orleans*. Their quarters were cramped, and they went for weeks without sighting land. They had decided to make the trip during the warm summer months when the sea was at its calmest, but they encountered a hurricane blowing itself out in the North Atlantic.

Tim's father said that when the little ship got into the trough between two giant waves they had to look up to see the crests of the waves. When they rode up a wave to its crest, they looked down into what seemed to be a bottomless canyon. At times during the storm, they did not think their little ship would make it through. But after three days of blowing, the waves smoothed out again. The skipper told them they had been very close to where they planned to dock off Massachusetts, but now the storm had blown them back out to sea and northward. Now they were somewhere off Newfoundland's Grand Bank.

They sailed southward again. There was no food left aboard the ship, but this time they made a safe landing on the coast of Massachusetts. Tim's father said that he and his wife never wanted to see a ship or the ocean again. That was the main reason they had moved so far inland.

Now Tim's father and mother were dead, and Tim was taking a trip on a boat. He had been so busy these past few months that he had not had time to think about his parents or to be sad, but now tears came to his eyes. He was glad no one could see him cry, but the crying did make him feel better.

The sky had begun to flush with dawn when Tim, his back to the rail, fell sound asleep. Tiger had joined him and slept with his head across Tim's legs.

An hour or so later Tim was awakened by loud shouting. At first he was stiff from his cramped position, but a bit of stretching limbered him almost immediately. Mr. Roosevelt was gathering the whole crew on deck. Ahead lay a tiny settlement on the north shore, and it looked as though everybody had come out to see the *New Orleans* steam by.

"Let's give them a wave," Mr. Roosevelt said.

The crew—some of whom had at first been only half-believers that the steamboat would work—gathered at the rail. Each man was now convinced that the *New Orleans* was a success, and each was proud to be a part of the boat. They waved and shouted enthusiastically as the boat sped by the settlement and its inhabitants.

Mr. Roosevelt opened the escape valve on the boiler to let out a hissing cloud of steam. At the same time, the engineer stoked the fire again to make the smoke roll and sparks fly out of the stack. All of this was to put on an exciting show for the little crowd gathered on shore, and they liked it. As a finale, Mr.

Roosevelt rang the big brass bell that hung in front of the pilothouse. He kept ringing it until they were far down the river and out of sight.

It was the morning of the second day when the *New Orleans* reached the dock in Cincinnati. Captain Jack turned the boat around in the current so that her prow pointed into the current, and they tied up. Before this was finished, a huge crowd had gathered. Among them were people that Mr. Roosevelt had talked to on his earlier expedition. He had promised them that he would come back by steamboat before the year was over. They agreed now that he had fulfilled his promise, but many of them still did not believe the steamboat was a practical idea.

"You're going *down* the river," they said, "and that's easy. The steam helps hurry you along some maybe. If you'd promised to come upstream to visit us, you'd have never made it."

Mr. Roosevelt smiled but did not argue. All he said was, "Gentlemen, the day will soon come when you will see steamboats coming up the Ohio River regularly."

The skeptics shook their heads.

Before the day was over, flatboatmen who had been passed by the *New Orleans* upstream the day before and during the night began arriving in Cincinnati. All of them had tales to tell about how the steamboat had sped past like she was being towed by sixty horses. Each added his bit of fiction to the fact. Most of them said the big boat had left giant waves in its wake. They said the waves had washed across their flatboats, smashed against the shore, and then headed back at them again. Some said the smoke from the big stack blinded them. Others worried that the sparks might set fire to their supplies. But no one was really injured. One and all agreed that the *New Orleans* was the biggest spectacle that had ever come to the river country. And almost every one of them doubted that the steamboat would ever replace the flatboat on the river.

Tim, Captain Jack, and the crew listened to the various tales and could only smile in response. They had once doubted what the *New Orleans* could do, too—but no more. The run from Pittsburgh to Cincinnati had taken all of the doubt out of them. They were now sure that steamboats had come to the river to stay. Further, Tim and the crew were too busy getting supplies aboard the *New Orleans* for the trip to Louisville to waste time with talk.

Late that afternoon, Captain Jack rang the bell to signal the crew that the *New Orleans* would soon depart. All was in readiness for the trip down the river to Louisville. Tim helped take in the lines, and then he and the crew pushed the *New Orleans* out into the river's channel.

"How about letting me tow you?" one of the flatboatmen shouted as he shoved past them.

"Yeah," a fellow on the dock chimed in, "and maybe they can hire you to pole them back upstream if they decide to come this way. That belcher will never make it on its own."

Captain Jack laughed.

The engineer opened the escape valve on the boiler to see if they had a head of steam. A cloud of mist hissed into the Indian summer air.

"Careful there," a man yelled from shore. "She's leakin' out all her power."

The *New Orleans* had now gotten out beyond the

cluster of flatboats near shore. Many of them were holding back, scared by the hissing. At Mr. Roosevelt's signal, the engineer pulled the lever that started the churning piston, and the big wheels began to revolve. Captain Jack turned the wheel, and almost as if she were on ice, the *New Orleans* spun around and pointed her prow downstream.

On shore the people forgot their doubts about the future of steamboating for a moment. A steamboat was here right now and was performing to perfection. As the *New Orleans* picked up speed, she passed the flatboat that had just pushed past her. The bearded riverboatman shrugged his shoulders as she steamed by. He had not made it to the mainstream yet.

Tim and the crew stood at the stern and waved goodbye to the people of Cincinnati.

CHAPTER FIVE

ON TO LOUISVILLE

A few miles down the river from Cincinnati Mr. Roosevelt suggested that they might put in for the night, then complete the run to Louisville the next day. Captain Jack wanted to continue, however. This was the stretch of the river that he knew best of all, for it was here that he got his start as a riverman. Mr. Roosevelt agreed to go ahead.

The river now ran wider, the shores less hugging. The autumn forests were ablaze with the bright reds of oaks, the yellows of hickories, and the rich browns of all those leaves that had already lost their colors and now hung on the trees waiting for a frost or a cold rain to tumble them to the ground. The day had been bright and warm, but with sunset came a cool hint of the winter weather to come.

Tiger had taken such a liking to Tim that he generally joined him on deck during his watches. For the first few days the big dog had been a bit

nervous on the boat, but now his legs were so firm under him that he walked straight and without a whimper even when the deck rolled slightly.

Most of the time when he was with Tim on watch he sat near the rail and studied the passing shore. Now and then he would whine or give a low growl. Then Tim would bend down to get his eyes level with the dog's to see what was exciting him. Sometimes it was a settler's prowling hound. Several times he spotted deer that had come to the shore for a drink and then paused, head lifted, to stare in wonder at the odd boat going by.

That evening the sun turned into a fiery ball that cast a blood-red trail over the river. The golden-red globe was like a glowing ember, not so bright that they could not look directly at it. For a long while it seemed to hang motionless at the horizon; then it dropped suddenly into the water. And after the sun itself had disappeared, a kaleidoscope of colored banners streamed across the sky.

The gray twilight that followed was filled with thousands of twinkling lights of fireflies. They danced over the river. Soon the frosts of autumn would cut them down. Like the *New Orleans*, great flocks of ducks and geese followed the wormlike course of the river toward the Mississippi. There the migrants would turn southward to find winter warmth. Shortly a big harvest moon rose in the east and cast a broad yellowish-orange path down the river behind them.

Now and then they could see from aboard the *New Orleans* the flickering light of a fire along the shore. As they neared Louisville, they saw more lights. It was nearly midnight when they arrived directly opposite Louisville. The town was mostly dark, the people asleep.

Captain Jack had let Tim take the wheel as he had several times now since they left Pittsburgh. "Spin her round about!" Captain Jack shouted from the prow. "Put her nose up current, and we'll drop anchor."

Tim spun the wheel. The *New Orleans* turned first shoreward and then poked her prow into the current.

"Drop anchor!" Captain Jack shouted.

Tim heard a splash.

"Too deep here," Captain Jack called. "Take her in a bit."

Tim turned her to the starboard and let the wheels churn the *New Orleans* closer to shore.

"Not too far, boy. Not too far. Shoals way out here. Turn her back, turn her back!"

Again Tim spun the wheel so the *New Orleans* was headed directly into the current.

The anchor held fast this time. The engineer pulled the big lever to cut the power of the piston driving the wheels. They slowed to a halt. The crew held the *New Orleans* in place with poles while Captain Jack splashed ashore with a line to secure the boat to the dock. The engineer opened the escape valve on the boiler to let the built-up steam escape. It rushed out with a loud hiss.

All of the shouting and the hissing steam had rousted people along the shore out of their beds. By the time all the lines were tied, crowds had gathered at the dock to find out what was happening. Some said they thought the Great Comet had come back and had fallen into the river right there at Louisville.

Early the next morning, a welcoming committee came to the *New Orleans* to greet Mr. Roosevelt. They remembered him from the year before. He had promised then to return to Louisville by steamboat, and they were delighted to see him.

"You've done exactly what you said you would do, Mr. Roosevelt," one of the men said. "You came down the river by steamboat. But you could never go against the current with your boat."

This was the same story they had heard in Cincinnati, and again, Mr. Roosevelt only smiled. Instead of disagreeing, he asked about the level of the river at the Falls of the Ohio, not far from Louisville. This was a mile or more of shallow, rippling, rocky water, the biggest hazard that lay between Louisville and where the Ohio emptied into the Mississippi. Flatboatmen who had just made the journey gave him their stories, and then he and Captain Jack talked it over soberly.

"We will have to lay over here in Louisville until the river rises some," Mr. Roosevelt said. "The water's too shallow right now for the *New Orleans* to make it over the rapids safely."

"We could move on downstream and wait there all ready to go," Captain Jack suggested, eager to keep on the move.

"But we must keep Mrs. Roosevelt's condition in mind," Mr. Roosevelt explained. The baby was about due, and Mr. Roosevelt had planned to be near a town and a doctor when the event happened. "With luck, we'll get the baby and the rain all within a week. Meanwhile we can keep the *New Orleans* in readiness. There's no place for us to stop between here and New Madrid."

That night the people of Louisville invited Mr. and Mrs. Roosevelt and the whole crew of the *New Orleans* to a grand feast and a dance in the town hall. It was a night Tim would never forget—both the feast and the fun.

With the harvest season just ended, larders were filled. There were venison, hams, fish, squirrels, doves, quail—every kind of fish, fowl, and meat the Louisville people could bring from the stores or get from the woods and waters. And there were corn, sweet potatoes, onions, tomatoes, squash, pumpkins, apples, pears—more food than Tim had ever seen in his whole life. After they had eaten their fill, the riverboatmen and the mountain men of Kentucky got their fiddles and started a hoedown. The singing and dancing went on until it was almost time for the sun to come up.

Before the party was over, Mr. Roosevelt made a speech. He addressed particularly the group of prominent Louisville men who had come out to the *New Orleans* to welcome him and had then put together the party. He invited them all aboard the *New Orleans* for dinner the next night. He explained that he would like to entertain everybody in Louisville as they had him and his crew but that the *New Orleans* simply wasn't as big as their town hall. He thanked all the people in Louisville for their hospitality and said maybe he would be back again someday with a boat big enough for everybody—if they would widen the river enough to let him through. The people laughed and cheered. Then Mr.

Roosevelt waved to the fiddlers to go on with the music so the people could dance.

Tim and the rest of the crew headed back to the *New Orleans*. They were all tired from their late run down the river the night before and then the big festivities of this evening.

But at sunup the next morning they were routed out of bed. Mr. Roosevelt wanted the *New Orleans* put in shipshape before the end of the day. Every inch of her was to be gone over with great care, for Mr. Roosevelt wanted her to look her very best when his Louisville visitors came aboard.

For food there was absolutely nothing to give their guests that had not been on the tables set for them the night before. Mr. Roosevelt said the people would understand this. He was sure they would be so excited about being aboard the steamboat that they would hardly know what they were eating anyhow. Tim helped put planks on sawhorses to make a long table that was set in the galley area.

That evening when the Louisville people arrived at the *New Orleans*, Mr. Roosevelt first took them on a complete tour of the boat. He explained how the steam engine worked and how much power it generated. The people listened with interest, but like the skeptics at Cincinnati, they told Mr. Roosevelt that he underestimated the strength of the current even in the Ohio. And no steamboat could ever match the might of the Mississippi.

With a smile, Mr. Roosevelt returned them to the table so that food could be served.

While they were eating, Mr. Roosevelt talked quietly and with that convincing authority that always put him in command of groups such as this. They listened almost spellbound as he explained what the steamboat might mean to their future. Soon steamboats would be common sights on both the Ohio and the Mississippi, he told them. They would bring cotton, sugar, and passengers up the river all the way from New Orleans. On the way back they would carry corn, wheat, and other products of the river country. But even those who listened almost in awe as Mr. Roosevelt talked more excitedly were privately sure that he was mostly just a dreamer.

Nearly everyone had finished his dinner when the *New Orleans* lurched and loud noises came from below the cabin.

"The boat's torn loose from her moorings," one of the men shouted. He rose excitedly and rushed from the galley. The others followed him, and they all gathered at the rail.

Tim was already there. Mr. Roosevelt had gotten his crew together much earlier to prepare for this stunt to surprise his guests. For the *New Orleans* had not broken loose at all, though indeed she was now headed out into the river. While the people were eating, the crew had quietly untied the steamboat and poled her away from the dock. Already they had drifted nearly a mile below Louisville.

The noise the diners heard was the sound of the boiler heating up—and then the engineer had opened the safety valve to let some of the steam hiss out. He had then pulled the lever to make certain the piston was operating to drive the wheels; this caused the lurch. Mr. Roosevelt had warned everyone that the reputation of the *New Orleans* and the future of steamboating on the Ohio would be given a strong measure by what happened that night in Louisville.

Mr. Roosevelt stepped from the galley and then climbed to the top of the pilothouse where he could be seen clearly in the moonlight. He checked first to see that all of his crew were at their stations. Then he turned to his guests.

"You are now a mile or so south of Louisville," he announced calmly. "To get you home again, the *New Orleans* must take you upstream. You will find out for yourselves whether the steamboat has strength enough to run against the river's full current."

The men from Louisville stood quietly at the rail. They had no choice but to let the *New Orleans* go to work to carry them home.

"We are ready, Captain Jack," Mr. Roosevelt shouted.

Captain Jack signaled the engineer. Familiar to Tim was a growling grind as the gears were engaged and the big wheels began to turn. The passengers remained silent. They watched the outline of the shore. Sure enough, the *New Orleans* began to move upstream. Then they shouted with glee.

Mr. Roosevelt climbed down to the deck, and the men from Louisville gathered around. Some of them now said that they had never really doubted the steamboat. Again, Mr. Roosevelt smiled without comment. He was satisfied that they now believed in steamboating. Among themselves the men began talking about what the steamboat would mean to business in Louisville. A new world was at their riverfront. The words that came from them were almost the same as those Mr. Roosevelt had used earlier, but now they belonged to the men of Louisville.

The current was strong, and the *New Orleans* labored—but she kept moving steadily. Soon the lights of Louisville began to flicker like fireflies along the shore.

People carrying torches had gathered at the dock where the *New Orleans* had been tied up. They wanted to know what had happened to the steamboat. They began to shout to their friends aboard. There was much joking and laughter, and the tale of the dinner aboard the *New Orleans* was told in many ways before the visitors got to shore. With each telling, too, the steamboat grew in stature, and along with her, Mr. Roosevelt and his crew.

spread the word in the taverns and along the streets that the *New Orleans* was on its way. By the time the steamboat was ready to pull in to shore to tie up, the bank was lined with people.

Quickly Mr. Roosevelt ran his eyes over the group. He hoped to see there some of those who had questioned whether the steamboat could ever travel upstream. And they were there—their mouths gaping.

First Mr. Roosevelt let his Louisville passengers go ashore. They were, in fact, his unquestionable proof that the *New Orleans* had gone that far downstream. Then he climbed atop the pilothouse, where everyone could see and hear him.

"The *New Orleans* has returned," he shouted so that the still-gathering crowd could hear him, "and for only one reason: to prove to the doubters that steam power has come to the West to stay. Before another year is past, you will be trading with Louisville, Natchez, and even New Orleans by steamboat. People will travel by steamboat, too. Steam power is the fast, sure way—and the only way to be master of the mainstream."

Cheers and applause came from the crowd. Some of the men who had been so critical of the *New Orleans* on the first stop at Cincinnati now stepped forward to shake Mr. Roosevelt's hand. He leaned down to accept their congratulations. After a few minutes, he stood up again and waved for silence from the milling crowd.

"We would like to stay longer," he said, "but the day is still much with us. With steam power added to the current, we might be back in Louisville before sundown. And we *must* get back soon. Anytime now my wife expects to present us with our second child. Boy or girl, we will have a child born of this new era of river travel—the steamboat days of the West."

The engineer opened the valve over the boiler to let out steam. There was a loud hiss, and the hot vapor made a giant cloud that swept over the stern of the *New Orleans*. The crowd waved wildly and shouted their good wishes as the boat was quickly untied. Tim joined the crew in poling the boat from the shallows out into the current. Smoke furled from the big boat's stack. Her flags waved merrily in the brisk, nippy wind. In less than half the time it had taken them to cover the same distance coming upstream, the big boat had rounded the bend that put Cincinnati out of sight.

Mr. Roosevelt had accomplished his mission. The skeptical Cincinnatians were now convinced that the steamboat had conquered the Ohio.

They made the return trip to Louisville speedily. Along the way they passed some of the same rafts and flatboats they had seen the day before.

"Wal, you got her workin' fer you now. Finally figured out which way the river runs," the rivermen chided.

For two weeks more the *New Orleans* lay at anchor just off Louisville. Each morning they searched the skies for signs of rain, but the sun always poked through the morning mists and left the sky clear. It was almost summery again with the sun often glowing like a hot coal in the strange gray-blue sky. Winter had begun normally, but now it had stopped.

At sunup one morning, Mr. Roosevelt came back

aboard the *New Orleans* from Louisville. He had taken his wife ashore to a doctor's house the evening before when it appeared that the baby was on the way.

"It's a boy," he announced through a proud smile. "We have named him Henry Latrobe Roosevelt."

Captain Jack joined the crew who had gathered around Mr. Roosevelt to give him their congratulations. After each had his turn, Captain Jack stepped forward.

"I have a report, too," he said. "The river is rising!"

The whole crew stomped on the deck and clapped each other on the back. Louisville had been fun and the people hospitable, but what had started out as a daily parade of exciting adventures had now come to a halt. They were bored and anxious to be on the move again.

Somewhere far upstream—perhaps as far away as Pittsburgh—the rains had been falling. Now the big river had begun to creep up bit by bit as her feeder stream flowed full again following the long, dry summer.

Each morning they checked the river, then again at noon, and once more before sundown. And each time they found the river a little bit higher.

On the fifth day, Mr. Roosevelt said the crew should have the *New Orleans* ready to leave Louisville the next morning. Already November was nearly gone, and he wanted to get the steamboat to her destination before a big freeze turned the river to ice. The *New Orleans* would not begin to pay off her cost until she began to ply between Natchez and New Orleans.

The crew set about getting more fuel aboard and

checking what supplies they needed to carry with them from Louisville. Mr. Roosevelt went ashore to get Mrs. Roosevelt and her baby. Mrs. Roosevelt brought back with her not only the baby but also a pretty young lady, Martha, who would be her maid to help care for the infant on the trip to Natchez. Tim noticed that Captain Jack seemed to take an immediate liking to the young woman. When he helped the two ladies aboard, he seemed almost unaware of Mrs. Roosevelt. And Mr. Roosevelt brought still another new member of the crew—a river pilot who knew the Falls of the Ohio and the river beyond.

Tiger had spent most of the days in Louisville curled in sleep near the galley. But now he seemed to sense the meaning of the sudden stir into action. He took up his post at the prow of the boat, ready for whatever adventure lay ahead.

CHAPTER SEVEN

OVER THE FALLS

Spirits were high aboard the *New Orleans* the morning they shoved off from Louisville and headed downstream. Yet they were sad, too, for they had gained many friends in Louisville during the weeks they were anchored there. Men shook Mr. Roosevelt's hand and made him promise to come back again. Women dabbed at tears as they waved to Mrs. Roosevelt. Like the women in Pittsburgh, they had tried to talk her into staying with them while the *New Orleans* made its maiden voyage into the West. But Mrs. Roosevelt still insisted that she and her newborn son should be with her husband.

Louisville was the last big town they would see before they reached Natchez. Just below the mouth of the Ohio, they would come to the old Spanish settlement of New Madrid. Below that was Little Prairie. But mostly the journey from Louisville to Natchez would take them through wilderness. Only

71

a few miles from Louisville were the Falls of the Ohio.

If Mr. Roosevelt's calculations were correct, the *New Orleans* would just barely skim over the rapids. His biggest worry was keeping the wheels from hitting rocks, for repairs would be difficult to make. By his figures, they should have about half a foot to spare if they could find the deepest water and then stay in it. But he had observed, too, that the river was no longer rising. The river had crested—as high as it would go before winter freezes made it solid from shore to shore. He decided to make the run the next morning in full daylight.

So early that evening they tied the *New Orleans* close to the north shore at a spot where Mr. Roosevelt said they should find piles of coal nearby for fuel. On his way down the river by flatboat, he had piled up coal wherever he thought their needs would be greatest. They had found nearly a dozen such piles since leaving Pittsburgh, but this would be the last. Coal was dirty to handle, but it burned longer than the wood they would be burning from now on.

Tim went ashore with the crew to find the coal. The pile was about half a mile closer to the rapids than where the *New Orleans* was tied, and so one of the crew went back to get Captain Jack to move the steamboat closer. In the silence while they waited, Tim and the other members of the crew could hear the roar of the Falls of the Ohio not far from them.

Suddenly the woods seemed to come alive with scurrying gray squirrels. Thousands of them came from the hills, some jumping from tree to tree and others scampering along the ground. All were headed in the general direction of the river. When they reached the shore, some of them jumped in and began to swim across. Others ran along the bank, but soon there were so many squirrels pouring out of the woods that they all jumped into the river. By the time the *New Orleans* arrived, the river at that point had became a sea of squirrels.

"We wanted coal, not squirrels," Mr. Roosevelt called out to them jokingly. "But both would be fine. The squirrels will make mighty fine eating."

Half the crew set about loading the coal. The others began to kill squirrels with clubs. Tim did not like loading coal. It was hard, dirty work. But he liked loading coal better than killing squirrels. He did not like to kill anything. Even when they were eating squirrels later that night, he found it difficult to forget them as they were when they were alive.

Tim asked one of the crew who had traveled the river many times before whether he had ever seen as many squirrels here before. The man told him that he had not, but he had heard about squirrel migrations like this. Some years the squirrels seemed to be especially abundant. When they ate all the food where they lived, they were forced to move to a new area. And if that part of the woods was also crowded with squirrels, the army moved on, now double in numbers. Soon thousands and thousands of squirrels would scramble through the woods. Riverboatmen had come to places in the Ohio in late autumn where they said they believed they could walk across the river on the backs of squirrels.

That night the rush of water at the Falls of the Ohio lulled everyone aboard the *New Orleans* into a deep sleep. They were wide awake and rested early the next morning, ready for the hard day ahead of them.

Mr. Roosevelt told his wife that the ride through the rapids would be rough and perilous. For the first time, he seemed to be agreeing with the people in Pittsburgh and Louisville who had thought it would be best for her not to try the trip at all. He suggested that she take the baby and go with her maid and one of the crew through the woods on shore to the other side of the rapids. There they could join the *New Orleans* again when she was in safe, calm water.

But Mrs. Roosevelt had no intention of leaving the boat. She assured her husband that she had complete faith in him and in the *New Orleans* and that she wanted to be a part of whatever happened.

The engineer fired the boiler to build a full head of steam. Thick black smoke rolled out of the stack. Mr. Roosevelt said it would be best to run the rapids under full power. This would give them the greatest control for steering the steamboat. The lines holding the *New Orleans* were untied, and she swung from shore into the now rapid current that swept them speedily toward the Falls. For the first time since the start of their trip, Tim was a bit scared.

Captain Jack stood at the prow of the *New Orleans* with the pilot. Though he had traveled the river all the way to New Orleans, he did not know it as well as he knew the portion from Cincinnati to Louisville. By working alongside the pilot, he would learn this part of the river, too.

Together the two men at the prow waved commands to the crewman at the wheel. The noise of the rushing water as the river narrowed now into a fast-flowing channel was added to the pounding of the engine's piston and the churning of the wheels. Voices could not be heard.

Gray, rocky cliffs rose on each side of the boat. Sometimes great wedges of rock hung out so far on each side of the boat that they nearly scraped the pilothouse. In some places the channel was so narrow that Tim feared they could never get through, but in these places the water ran deeper and faster. The boat seemed to leap clear of the water, the big wheels spinning momentarily in air with nothing firm against which to push. Then the front would smack the water again with a crash that echoed from the walls of rocks.

Crewmen tried to use their poles to push the boat away from the shore when she seemed to get too close, but the *New Orleans* always whipped by these spots before they could get their poles into action. Clearly the boat was largely at the mercy of the river and the crewman at the wheel. Soon they simply held onto anything firm as the boat sped onward. They all felt that this was surely the end of their journey.

Suddenly the *New Orleans* spun into a broad, quiet pool. On the far side, a giant sandbar from the wash of the rapids lay shining in the sunlight. The rapids were behind them now. They had passed what Mr. Roosevelt had told them would be the greatest hazard of their journey. In a normal year, the Falls would not have been so treacherous, but the year 1811 was unusual—with more yet to come. The year had begun with floods, then the summer had been hot and dry. The Ohio was carrying much less water than usual. With higher water, many of the rough spots in the rapids would have been smoothed out.

Tiger had made the trip through the rapids crouched at Tim's feet. Occasionally he had whimpered. Now he rose and wagged his tail, sensing that the danger lay behind them. But now they were entering an untamed land of untamed people.

Fortunately, Mr. Roosevelt was too cunning to be caught in the trap that lay just ahead of them. He had heard tales about Cave-in-the-Rock, and he believed them enough to be on guard.

It was toward evening when they heard a woman's voice hailing them from shore. She stood on a jutting rock waving a white cloth. Mr. Roosevelt ordered the engine stopped so that they could hear what she was shouting.

"Cap'n! Cap'n!" she called loud and clear. "Lord praise you, we need your help. My husband and little girl are here in the woods ill. Would you send some men to fetch them aboard so's we can get to New Madrid? We need a doctor."

Mrs. Roosevelt urged her husband to help the woman.

"Bring them to the shore," Mr. Roosevelt yelled to the woman. Quietly he told his wife not to be too anxious.

"I cain't do that, Cap'n," the woman answered. "They ain't fit to bring themselves, and I can't carry them. Please, Cap'n. We need help."

Tim could not understand why Mr. Roosevelt did not send some of the crew ashore. "I'll go help bring them," he said, remembering how ill his own father and mother had been.

"Hold back, boy," Mr. Roosevelt said firmly. "This woman is a decoy."

Then he shouted to the woman again. "You come aboard and wait while I send my men to get them."

"But I got to show them where to go," the woman answered.

Mr. Roosevelt told her his crew could follow whatever directions she gave. It was obvious now that the woman was becoming upset with Mr. Roosevelt for being so cautious.

"Ain't you never been sick, Cap'n?" the woman taunted. "Didn't you ever need help from some other human to bring you around? Don't you have no mercy? Please, Cap'n," she coaxed.

"I've been ill all right," Mr. Roosevelt fired back. "But I've never been so sick that I could get a cure at Cave-in-the-Rock." He turned to Captain Jack and ordered him to start the engine again.

That woman, he explained, had been planted there to lure the crew ashore. He was not absolutely sure, but he guessed she was a member of the pirate outlaws who lived at Cave-in-the-Rock just around the next bend.

If he sent members of his crew ashore, they would never come back. Somewhere out of sight in the woods they would be attacked and killed by the pirates. After a time, if he had been gullible, he would send more of the crew looking for them, and they would be killed, too. By this time there would be so few left on the boat that the pirates could capture it with ease.

The woman had worked this trick or variations of it on many men traveling the river by raft or by flatboat. A few had escaped, however, and had warned the regulars on the river to beware of treachery at Cave-in-the-Rock.

As the *New Orleans* steamed back into the main channel, Mr. Roosevelt told his men to get their guns ready. "We may have uninvited guests just after we round the next bend," he said. The woman had suddenly disappeared from the rock where she had been standing.

Mrs. Roosevelt took her baby and went into her cabin. The maid joined her.

Again Mr. Roosevelt proved to be wise. Just as they rounded the next bend, they saw two skiffs shoot out into the river from beneath a bluff. In each there were three men with guns. Mr. Roosevelt said the cave was hidden somewhere in the trees on the side of the bluff. This was their stronghold, where they lived and kept their booty.

Before the men were really close enough to be harmed, Mr. Roosevelt ordered his crew to fire a volley of shots. He knew the shots would fall short of their targets, but he wanted to let the pirates know they were headed for a fight. At the same time he told the engineer to give the *New Orleans* all the power he could get from the engine.

The *New Orleans* roared and belched and sped past the astonished pirates, who sat in their skiffs in awe at the sight of the steamboat. This was a prize bigger than they had really imagined, and it left them in no spirit for fighting. As they drank their liquor during the long winter nights ahead, they would talk about this big one that got away.

Tim moved to the stern of the *New Orleans* to watch the drifting skiffs until they became small dots behind them. There was another hour's running time before they tied up for the night, and in only one more day they should be entering the Mississippi.

CHAPTER EIGHT

THE WILDERNESS

As the *New Orleans* got closer to the great Mississippi, the land changed. All the way down the Ohio from Pittsburgh to Louisville, there had scarcely been a time when those aboard could not see the smoke from a cabin. Small settlements dotted the shore. Nearly always a raft or a flatboat could be seen somewhere on the river.

But now they were in the West. The steep hills of the Ohio Country had begun to level off into deep, dark lowlands of dense forests. Often they traveled for hours without seeing any evidence that anyone had ever been in this part of the world before. To Tim it was eerie, almost frightening. But the rivermen who had made the trip before knew the way and spotted familiar landmarks.

Wild creatures were much more abundant here in the wilderness. Mr. Roosevelt told Tim that soon he would see more birds than he believed lived in the

whole world. And it happened that afternoon.

The *New Orleans* had been tied up while the crew went ashore to get wood. These stops were more frequent now than when they used the coal that Mr. Roosevelt had piled along the shore on his trip down the river. The wood burned much faster. While they were cutting wood, Tim and the crew heard a roaring noise in the northwest. They turned to see what caused it. Passenger pigeons—dovelike birds—began to drop in from the sky and settle in the trees along the shore. And that first cloud of birds was simply a hint of the great whirring of wings that followed them. So many passenger pigeons came in to roost that they literally blotted out the sun and darkened the sky. Sometimes so many birds would try to get on the same branch that it broke from their weight and crashed to the ground. The birds would rise, colliding with other flocks that were trying to land.

Soon there were so many birds and so much noise that the crew of the *New Orleans* had to shout at each other to be heard. Tiger barked in a deep, hoarse voice. Tim stared in wonder.

Mr. Roosevelt ordered the crew to kill enough birds to give them a supply of food. They could easily fill the boat's larder for several days of travel. Some pigeons could be put in barrels and salted down for eating later. Again Tim shied from the killing. He continued to cut wood while others in the crew went about the bloody harvest.

Sunset was still hours away, but the sky continued to be darkened by the birds. There seemed to be no end to the flock—millions and millions of fluttering, chortling passenger pigeons. Tim was happy when Mr. Roosevelt ordered the boiler fired up so they could be on their way again. He was anxious to escape the noise.

The scream of the steam from the boiler and the billows of smoke from the stack set the birds off again. They rose from their roosts, each disturbing two or three others. The steamboat plowed its way through a flutter of feathers to the main channel. When Tim looked back toward the shore, he saw that the ground had suddenly turned white. The droppings looked like snow beneath the trees where the birds were roosting. And the clamor of the birds could be heard even above the noise of the steamboat.

Tim agreed with Mr. Roosevelt that he had now seen more birds than he had ever thought he would. He was glad when the world around them became almost silent again, with only the churning of the wheels and the thumping of the piston. Now they sounded so quiet!

The *New Orleans* moved steadily down the river. Tim and the crew began to talk about the Mississippi now. It lay just ahead. They had just finished dressing the pigeons, salting some down and keeping others to be eaten fresh, when they heard a loud shout from Captain Jack in the pilothouse. They jumped to their feet.

"Indians!" Captain Jack shouted again.

Tim looked down the river and saw two canoes moving out rapidly from the south shore. In each canoe there were four Indians. Two more canoes soon followed them. They were armed with guns and were headed directly for the *New Orleans*.

"Get your guns," Mr. Roosevelt yelled. "They are attacking. Begin firing as soon as they get close enough."

Captain Jack lifted his gun from just behind the wheel in the pilothouse and leveled it toward the nearest canoe. He fired, and the Indian at the front of the canoe lurched and grabbed at his shoulder.

Then the engineer fired from the galley window, and the Indian at the back of the canoe bent double. With both of its paddlers now wounded, the canoe swerved. The two Indians in the middle tried to recover the floating paddles. In the process the canoe upset. The canoes following it stopped to help. Meanwhile the *New Orleans* was moving ahead rapidly. The Indians whooped and brandished their guns, but the big boat was much too fast for them.

Ahead now, with the setting sun streaming across it like a golden highway, the river suddenly broadened. Here the Ohio joined the Mississippi. The *New Orleans* steamed toward the northern shore and tied up for the night.

Everyone gathered on deck to have a last look at the sun. It was strangely ominous, unlike any evening they had ever seen. That night they slept with more than the usual anxieties.

In the middle of the night they were suddenly awakened by a violent shaking of the boat. It seemed as though the big boat had been literally picked up from the water by a great monster. Tim was thrown from his bunk, and he lay there for a few minutes trying to collect his thoughts. He was not fully awake when he heard the shout.

"Fire!"

The shaking of the boat, whatever had caused it, had thrown coals from the firebox into the tinder nearby. The dry wood had quickly blazed, and the fire was now creeping toward the walls. All hands were on deck immediately, dipping water from the river to put out the flames. Everyone's thoughts at the moment were on the fire. Little was said about the shaking of the ship.

But the fire was no sooner put out than the shaking began again. The earth rolled and rocked, tipping first in one direction and then another. Great waves came up the river and shook the *New Orleans*, just as though she were riding a stormy sea. It was frightening. Tim became sick to his stomach. Time after time the earth shook during the night. Nobody even tried to sleep again.

Tim was glad when a glow in the eastern sky told them dawn was coming. Mr. Roosevelt ordered them to get underway, hoping that whatever was causing the shaking would soon be behind them. Little did he know that he was heading the *New Orleans* directly toward the heart of the strongest earthquake ever to strike the North American continent.

CHAPTER NINE

THE RIVER FLOWS UPSTREAM

The day was cloudy, and snow spit from the heavy sky. Mr. Roosevelt and Captain Jack both stood at the prow of the *New Orleans*, studying the big Mississippi down which the boat was moving rapidly. Tim, at the wheel in the pilothouse above them, could hear what they said.

"The lowlands are flooded all right," Mr. Roosevelt remarked. "Look there at the driftwood back in the trees. I'd guess the river's up half a foot or more."

"What do you make of it, sir?" Captain Jack asked.

"Well, we obviously had an earthquake right here last night. And thank goodness we are putting it behind us now."

But all that day they moved through the grayness seeing more signs of the quake. They had expected to ride a strong current in the Mississippi, but instead, the current was sluggish. Yet from all the indications the big river was on the rise. It was all

very strange. Darkness seemed to come in the middle of the afternoon, and before the pitch of night was upon them, Mr. Roosevelt had the *New Orleans* swung toward the shore and tied to the bank so the crew could cut wood.

While they were off in the woods cutting, several straggling bands of settlers passed through and stopped to talk. They were leaving the region, frightened by the shaking of the ground the night before.

One man said he had built his cabin on the bank of a small stream that fed into the Mississippi. During the night, he and his wife were awakened by the violent shaking of the cabin. It seemed to rise and fall, like a ship in a heavy sea—and then suddenly it slid from the bank right into the stream. Trees toppled over with it.

He and his wife had climbed out of the cabin and back onto shore, spending the remainder of the night huddled in the old cabin clearing while time after time the earth shook and trees fell all around them. They counted more than two dozen tremors. They were tempted to take refuge in a cave under a cliff nearby, but fortunately they did not. In the morning light they discovered there was no cliff. The whole side of the hill had slipped over it.

Cold and half-believing the earth was coming to an end, the couple had begun wandering through the woods toward Louisville. They warned Mr. Roosevelt that the *New Orleans* was headed in the wrong direction. Whatever had happened seemed worse to the south, they said—nearer to New Madrid. But they agreed, too, that it was probably now all over.

Mr. Roosevelt listened to the various stories. Some of the settlers asked to be taken aboard. They felt that the boat might be safer than the land. To them, it was like Noah's ark. But Mr. Roosevelt refused. He said he must move ahead toward New Madrid rather than returning to Louisville. He assured them that from all he knew about earthquakes, they had no more to worry about. The earthquake had come the night before, and there would be no more.

That night they tied to an island in the middle of the river. From their experience with falling trees the night before, it seemed best to stay out in the middle of the river in case the earthquake did happen to be repeated. And it did come again—later this time, almost at dawn. But the shakes this time were even worse than the first. Several times the prow of the *New Orleans* was lifted while her stern was still in the water. Then the prow would dip and the stern would go high in the air.

Tim heard Mrs. Roosevelt's maid sobbing in her cabin. From his few treasured personal belongings, he took the Bible from which he and his mother had read earlier in the year during desperate hours. When the tremors subsided, he carried the Bible to Martha's cabin and knocked on the door.

"It's Tim," he called out. "I have something for you."

The young woman opened the door and Tim slipped the Bible into her hand. In her other hand she held a candle, and by its flickering light Tim could see her tear-streaked face.

"Read the places with marks," Tim told her. "They will put you at ease."

"Thank you," Martha replied softly, shutting the door again.

Tim made his way back to the stern where he sat with Tiger, waiting for dawn to come.

When it was light enough, Mr. Roosevelt said they should begin to move ahead. The river was acting peculiar, and he wanted to get power under the boat so they could keep away from floating trees.

"Look here, Mr. Roosevelt," Captain Jack yelled. "We lost our island."

Sure enough, the island where they anchored that night had disappeared. During the upheavals, it had dissolved in the river like salt.

"And Mr. Roosevelt," Captain Jack added, with almost a chill in his voice, "we seem to have rounded about."

"What do you mean?" Mr. Roosevelt asked.

"I mean, sir, that we have either rounded about or the river is flowing in the wrong direction."

Both men studied the sky to be sure where in the darkness of the strange day the sun should be. The *New Orleans* had stood her ground all right. So there was only one answer: the mighty Mississippi was really flowing upstream!

By good fortune they had taken on an extralarge supply of fuel the night before. Mr. Roosevelt now ordered the fire to be built to get a head of steam. Meanwhile he and Captain Jack continued to study the strange direction the river was flowing.

"I am sure that is the direction we must go," Mr. Roosevelt pointed. "That is downstream, yet the river right now is flowing toward us."

Nearly an hour passed before the two men decided

that the Mississippi was very slowly righting itself. They untied the *New Orleans* and steamed down the river—now with the current coming from behind them as it should.

"Let's make it to New Madrid before nightfall," Mr. Roosevelt ordered. "We'll find out there what's happening."

New Madrid stood on a bluff on the west bank of the Mississippi. When Mr. Roosevelt passed through the area earlier, more than seven hundred people lived in the thriving settlement. The town had been laid out by the Spaniards as a semifortress to control river traffic coming down from the Ohio Country. It had broad streets and several public squares. Here Mr. Roosevelt planned to provision the *New Orleans* for her run to Natchez. Between the two towns there was only one more sizable settlement—Little Prairie, a cluster of cabins in a lowland meadow.

As they neared New Madrid they saw rafts, flatboats, and skiffs struggling upstream. The people in them hardly gave the steamboat a glance. They stared ahead, looks of horror on their faces. For the first time in their journey, Mr. Roosevelt stood on deck trying to hail the people but got no response. And now even the crew of the *New Orleans* had become almost totally silent. They looked at the devastated, toppled world along the shore and at the strangely silent people—and they wondered why Mr. Roosevelt persisted in moving toward what was obviously the center of the catastrophe.

"New Madrid is just around the next bend," Mr. Roosevelt announced solemnly, his voice almost echoing.

Silently the crew watched the view that came to them as they swung the *New Orleans* around the next bend. Even Mr. Roosevelt gasped at the sight. New Madrid was gone!

All that remained of the once bustling settlement were two very sturdily built cabins, and both of them were shaken askew. The others were all in a shambles, several of them totally burned as a result of having fallen into the fires their inhabitants had built to keep themselves warm. Several great chasms crept from the river bank as far into the forested hills as they could see. In the chasms were jumbled trees, cabins, and rocks.

Captain Jack steered the *New Orleans* close to shore where a small cluster of people had gathered. At the sight of the smoke-belching steamboat, some of the people fled. They were afraid that this might be the monster that had caused their world to fall around them. Others came down to the shore and asked to be taken aboard. Mr. Roosevelt again told them he did not have space for passengers and that it was possible he was heading into worse conditions. He explained that it seemed to get worse the farther down the river he went and that he was headed for Natchez. He asked if they had heard from anyone downstream. The replies he got were hardly understandable. The people were much too frightened. All they really wanted was a "wing" under which to hide themselves while the world continued to shake itself to pieces.

The crew stood by silently until Mr. Roosevelt ordered them to pole away from the shore. The *New Orleans* steamed away. Tim looked back at the wreckage. He was almost afraid to look ahead at what might be worse.

CHAPTER TEN

MORE TROUBLE AHEAD

Trouble had begun the day the *New Orleans* got around the Falls of the Ohio. Now there seemed to be no letup. Once the whole crew had been jovial and confident. Now they were usually quiet, or they talked in low tones. Always they were alert for another shaking of the steamboat or of the ground on which they stood when they were ashore cutting wood.

Soon after they left New Madrid, it came time to take on fuel again. As usual Mr. Roosevelt had them turn the *New Orleans* with her prow pointed upstream. Then half the crew went ashore with axes. The others stayed aboard to keep watch and to do whatever had to be done to ready the *New Orleans*.

Tim worked in the woods, cutting and carrying. Captain Jack joined him. They worked side by side, and for a long while neither of them spoke. Finally Tim broke the silence. "Still trying to figure out

He got no further, for at this point there came a piercing shriek from the direction of the boat. He and Captain Jack raced back to the *New Orleans*.

Martha and Mrs. Roosevelt had come off the boat to walk along the bank. They often did this while the crew was cutting wood. It gave them a chance to exercise, and they liked the feeling of solid ground under their feet again. But this time when they turned to go back to the boat, they found three Indians blocking their path. It was Martha who had screamed.

As soon as he saw the trouble, Mr. Roosevelt called to the others of the crew to get their guns. When Tim, Captain Jack, and the woodcutters arrived, they found the Indians standing there calmly, their arms folded. They had made no attempt to do harm. One of them lifted his hands and stepped forward, beginning to talk as he did so. He spoke good English. What the Indians wanted, he explained, was to be taken aboard the steamboat to see how it operated. They hoped they might travel on down the river on the steamboat. He called the boat "penelere," meaning "fire canoe," and he said they had heard much about her long before her arrival.

Word passed down the river from Indian camp to Indian camp about the coming of the steamboat. The Indians had assumed, like many others, that the fire-belching boat had something to do with the fiery comet that had streaked across the sky earlier in the year. Perhaps this was the form the comet had taken once it had landed. And when the earth began to tremble, they were even more certain that the steamboat was the cause. They believed that the gray days were due to the smoke from the boat's stack, and the shaking of the earth resulted from the constant pounding of the big river by the wheels.

The tales had been told and retold until the steamboat became a symbol of all the evil that had fallen over their land. First they had thought they should destroy her, as the small band had attempted earlier. But then their fear became so great that they simply watched in awe as she steamed past. They would send the news down the river that the spirit of evil was on its way.

Why were these three Indians not afraid? Two of them were, the spokesman explained. They came with him only because they were his friends and trusted him. And he was unafraid because he had learned from a white man more than a year earlier about the steamboats in the East. He was surprised to find one in the West. He was willing to get aboard for a ride. He also wanted to get away from the shaking land.

Mr. Roosevelt explained that they had no space. He told the Indians how many people along the river had been turned away. Then he asked about the earthquake. He wanted to know if the Indians knew whether conditions would be worse farther south on the river.

The Indian told him he was not sure but that he believed the town of Little Prairie had also been destroyed, like New Madrid. Beyond that he knew nothing. But in the backcountry he said the earth had opened up in places and swallowed whole forests. Great waves of the river had swept through thickets and cropped them as close as if they had been cut by a scythe. In other places, the trees were bent by the weight of the rushing water and then shaken by the quake. Their branches became so entangled that they could not right themselves. They became a twisted mat through which no man or beast could move.

Much land, the Indians related, had simply seemed to sink into the earth. Water filled in the holes and was still there. Not far from where they stood, a great lake now covered a vast lowland where many of their people had once lived. After much shaking and rippling, the land had dropped into the earth. Then the river flowed in and covered the lowered land. In some places, the lake was fifty feet deep or more, and it was a hundred miles long and nearly half as wide in spots. The Indians who had lived there fled to higher ground when the shaking started.

Mr. Roosevelt told the Indians again that he was sorry he could not take them aboard. He thanked them for their information. Tim and Captain Jack then joined other members of the crew in loading their fuel aboard the boat. The Indians watched solemnly.

The *New Orleans* was untied and shoved out into the channel. There she drifted with the current while the engineer stoked the fire to build up the steam. Then, with the hiss and the grind that signaled the wheels were being engaged, the *New Orleans* again began to steam down the Mississippi.

It was clear and cold, but a soft breeze was blowing up the river. The earth now seemed settled and normal again.

CHAPTER ELEVEN

TO NATCHEZ!

Little Prairie, a day and a half's journey below New Madrid, lay in ruins. Unlike New Madrid, Little Prairie had no place to slide. It was located in a rich lowland that the rampant river had filled and covered over with mud and sand. All the people were gone.

The proud forests that once rimmed each side of the river were now tangles of branches and trunks. But the shaking, which had started on the night of December 16, had stopped now for two days. The crew was feeling a bit relaxed again, and they began to joke about what they would do when they reached Natchez. Tim remembered his talk with Captain Jack, and he wondered if he had gotten up nerve enough yet to ask Martha to marry him. He wanted to find out but decided it was something Captain Jack probably wished he had never discussed with him.

Tim had new thoughts now himself. Soon, if all went well, he would be in Natchez where he would have to find his aunt. A new life would start for him there, too. Or if Mr. Roosevelt allowed him, he might stay aboard and work on the *New Orleans* on her trips from Natchez to New Orleans and back.

Half a day past Little Prairie, Captain Jack suddenly called excitedly to Mr. Roosevelt. He and the pilot had lost the channel. All signs were gone, and the river seemed to be wandering through a maze of islands. What had appeared to be deep water suddenly showed the stumps of giant trees. They had somehow completely lost the river and were now moving over a submerged forest.

All of the crew gathered on deck to help steer, poling the boat away from trees and rocks and shouting when they found a strong current or any other indication of the main channel. Several flatboats came by, but the rivermen aboard were no help. They had lost their way, too. The great Mississippi had changed its course due to the earthquake.

The crew turned the *New Orleans* around and dropped anchor while Captain Jack and Mr. Roosevelt talked about this newest predicament. Obviously there was no reason to turn back. They had no place to go and could never again find the channel that had led them into this watery woodland anyhow. Their only hope was in working their way out— assuming the big river later collected itself for a more normal course.

With the steam power cut off and the wheels disengaged, they drifted. They hoped this would lead them to the main current. For what seemed like hours the crew poled and probed until at last the banks on either side grew firm again. The steam was built up, the wheels engaged, and the *New Orleans* was once again on its way.

Christmas Day of 1811 was spent on the Mississippi. All day long they had to remind themselves of what the day was, and except for their own words, they had no way of knowing. They spent the entire day just as they would any other—keeping the *New Orleans* in the main channel headed for Natchez, the capital of the Territory of Mississippi. And they kept going because at each bend of the river they found less evidence of the earthquake. Day by day, the scenery began to take on its normal look, and the weather became warmer—almost balmy.

Tim remembered the Christmas of the year before. He and his mother and father were still in their cabin.

On Christmas eve Tim and his father had cut a small cedar tree, nailed it to a block, and taken it into the cabin. There they decorated it with strings of popcorn, some colorful gourds, and ears of corn. On Christmas morning, Tim had found a present under the tree—a pair of socks that his mother had made for him. There was also a pair for his father. Tim wondered when she had done the work, for neither of them had seen her knitting. Neither he nor his father had presents for her or for each other, but both said this year would be different. Tim had no idea then just how different his world would become during the year of 1811.

It was the day after Christmas when they stopped for more fuel and Mrs. Roosevelt said she wanted to take a short walk on shore with her baby. She asked

Tim to accompany her, and Tiger was anxious to go with them. Mrs. Roosevelt said she would be more comfortable having a man along, and she also needed a companion for Tiger. She knew that wherever Tim went, Tiger would want to go too.

"You can call me Lydia," Mrs. Roosevelt told Tim as they walked along.

Tim tried, but it seemed strange to him. He liked polite formality. He told Mrs. Roosevelt his preference.

"I hope our Henry grows up to be just like you," Mrs. Roosevelt said seriously. "No one could ask for a finer son."

Tim felt a deep blush. Quickly he turned her attention to Tiger, who was busily digging into the rocks and loose dirt at the base of a tree.

"Looks like he's really after something," Tim said. He hurried to the dog's side and began helping him pull out dirt and rocks. Suddenly Tiger began to whimper. Obviously he was getting close to whatever was buried there.

Mrs. Roosevelt, with her baby cradled in her arms, stood far enough back to be out of the way of the flying dirt. Tim kept working with Tiger.

"There it is! There it is!" Tim shouted. "It's a big rattlesnake!"

Fortunately the snake was still stiff from the cold. The weather had warmed, but the warmth had not reached down to the depth where the snake had crawled to hibernate. Tim grabbed it by the tail and jerked it away from the excited dog.

"Call Tiger quick," he yelled. "The snake might warm up enough to bite."

Mrs. Roosevelt called Tiger to her side. The big

dog really did not want to go, but he was well trained and obedient. He sat down as she commanded but kept an excited watch to see what Tim was doing with his find.

Tim had no alternative but to kill the snake. He did not like to kill anything, but he made an exception in the case of a poisonous snake. They were dangerous, and he had to think of Tiger's welfare also. With the axe he had carried along he cut off the snake's head. Then he buried both the head and the body in the hole Tiger had dug, tamping the dirt in place with a piece of broken limb. When Mrs. Roosevelt told him he could join Tim, Tiger went over to inspect what had been done. He made no attempt to dig out the dead snake.

Slowly now they walked back to the *New Orleans*. Mrs. Roosevelt thanked Tim for getting rid of the snake.

"It was Tiger that stirred up the trouble," Tim said. "If it hadn't been for him, we'd have never known the snake was there, and it would still be sleeping. That snake was almost stiff as a poker from the cold weather we've had. If he'd come out into the sun these past few days, he could have given us a worrisome time. Truth is, though, we probably never would have seen him. He'd have heard us coming through the brush a long time before we got near him and then crawled off in the other direction. Snakes don't look for trouble. They just take care of themselves if trouble finds them."

"Maybe we should learn a lesson from them," Mrs. Roosevelt commented. "When we think trouble is headed our way, we should go off in the other direction."

"You mean we should have turned the *New Orleans* around and headed back to Louisville?" Tim asked, thinking about the problems they had encountered since leaving Louisville.

"No. We never knowingly headed into trouble," Mrs. Roosevelt justified, "but we certainly left a lot of it behind us. From now on, everything will go smoothly."

"I hope so," Tim agreed.

They were back at the *New Orleans* now, and Mrs. Roosevelt had a tale to tell her husband and the crew. They listened but at the same time continued getting ready to move on. As they traveled southward, they began to come across more flatboats and rafts poling up the river. Or sometimes the steamboat overtook them on the way down. Every night they tied up.

It was the second day of January when the *New Orleans* reached Natchez. Word of her arrival had already been passed along, and more than a thousand people were along the shore to greet her. Natchez was truly a magnificent sight, with its great mansions on the high bluff overlooking the river. In a strip of lowland under the bluff were clusters of rafts and flatboats and also many less pretentious homes.

As the *New Orleans* approached the landing site, Mr. Roosevelt had her swung around with her nose upstream, then ordered the wheels engaged to pull the boat into place. But the engineer had let the steam go down. The *New Orleans* drifted back into the mainstream and away from Natchez. The cheering crowd suddenly broke into laughter.

Quickly the engineer built up the fire. The *New*

Orleans' stack heaved smoke, and shortly the steam hissed from the escape valve. Then slowly but surely the steamboat labored against the current to the dock at Natchez. Captain Jack steered her to her mooring.

Mr. Roosevelt quickly jumped to the top of the pilothouse to say a few words to the wildly cheering crowd.

"People of Natchez," he shouted, "we have just demonstrated the power of the steamboat against the might of the Mississippi. You have seen now that we are the masters. And it is only fitting that you should see the *New Orleans* coming in to dock from downstream—from New Orleans. We will make that trip on a regular schedule starting next month."

There was applause. Mr. Roosevelt lifted his arms to silence the crowd.

"The steamboat brings you a new way of life. No longer will you have to work in the fields and then work against the river's current, too. The *New Orleans* is here to carry you and your products. It will make life easier here in the West, just as the steamboat is already doing throughout the East."

Again the people applauded.

"I have only one more thing to say," Mr. Roosevelt went on. "Our trip from Pittsburgh was both pleasant and frightful. We regret the great damage done to the land and settlements by the earthquake farther up the Mississippi. You should be grateful that you were blessed by not having it here.

"One pleasure of our trip is yet to come. Our captain, who will also be in charge of the trips from here to New Orleans, wants to take a bride. He wants his marriage to be aboard the *New Orleans* tomorrow, right here at the dock in Natchez. His bride will be the charming girl who was my wife's attendant since the birth of our baby in Louisville. Our boy, Henry Latrobe Roosevelt, was born on a steamboat and traveled through a land of earthquakes to come to Natchez. Captain Jack and Martha lived through those days of terror, and their children, too, will in all probability be steamboaters from Natchez."

Captain Jack and Martha were lifted to the top of the pilothouse so the crowd could see them and give them their good wishes. When they got down, Martha came immediately to Tim.

"For our marriage vows," she said, "we would like very much to use the Bible you gave me to read that horrible night up the river. It brought me much comfort."

Tim said he would be proud to have her use his Bible. And he knew his mother would have been pleased, too, that her book would start this young couple on their marriage trip.

Standing at the rail, Tim searched the faces of the Natchez people, wondering if his aunt looked like his mother. How would he recognize her? All of a sudden he was filled with excitement about finding a family again.

"Mr. Roosevelt," Tim said when the crowd had begun to go away and Mr. Roosevelt had a free minute, "I thank you for the ride and hope my services paid my fare. I want to go now to find my aunt. No matter whether I find her, I would still like a job aboard the *New Orleans* when you begin your regular runs. Do I have a chance?"

"Lad," Mr. Roosevelt began, almost fatherly, "you have more than earned your fare. You have money due you when we settle up in a few days. And you are a permanent part of the crew aboard the *New Orleans* if you'd like. I should not have called you a lad, either. You have proved yourself to be quite a young man."

Tim fidgeted in embarrassment but managed a thanks to Mr. Roosevelt. He told him he would be getting his personal belongings off the *New Orleans* as soon as he found his aunt—something he intended to do as quickly as he could. From aboard the *New Orleans* after they docked, he had seen a general store sign not far down the street. He was sure the storekeeper would know his aunt's whereabouts.

"What kin I git fer you, boy?" the storekeeper greeted him.

"Right now all I need is some information," Tim replied. "I want to know if you can tell me where Wilma and John Blake live here in Natchez. She's my aunt."

"You're a mite late, boy," the storekeeper answered. "They used to live here, but they're not here anymore. Fine folks they were, too."

Not even the earthquake had jolted Tim more than what the storekeeper had just told him. Crestfallen disbelief swept across his face.

"Son, you look like this news hits you real hard," the storekeeper said, his tone sympathetic. "Finding these folks meant a lot to you, I take it."

"Yes, sir," Tim told him honestly. Then he explained why he had been aboard the *New Orleans* on its first trip on the Mississippi. "Can you tell me how long they have been gone, and do you know where they went?"

"Left early last summer, as I recollect," the store-keeper began. "Had an itch to do some pioneering— both of them. They heard about a new settlement down off Florida. An island called Indian Key. So one day they packed up and headed for New Orleans. There they planned to get passage on a boat that would carry them down around the tip of Florida to the island."

"Do you know if they got there all right?" Tim thought they might possibly still be in New Orleans, where he could soon travel on the steamboat.

"Yep, I do. A fellow from New Orleans stopped in here not so long ago, and he'd been to Indian Key. Said they liked it a lot. Palm trees, fish, no winter... and they are busy workin' with some doctor— Perrine, I believe is his name—who collects plants from Mexico and places like that. He grows 'em in plots on the island to see if they'd be good crop plants. Plans to start a big plantin' operation up on the mainland as soon as trouble with the Indians gets settled. The government gave him lots of land."

"Thank you," Tim said. "This was not the news I expected or wanted, but you have told me what I need to know. I guess I will be heading to Indian Key, too, but that may take a bit of doing."

Tim left the store and made his way slowly back toward the *New Orleans*. Reaching Natchez had fulfilled part of his promise to his mother, but he